A guide to

Rape Awareness and Prevention

A guide to

Rape Awareness and Prevention

*Educating yourself, your family
and those in need*

by

Robert and Jeanine Ferguson

T   Turtle Press   Hartford

Photographs by Beverly Slayton

To contact the author or order additional copies of this book:

Turtle Press
401 Silas Deane Hwy.
PO Box 290206
Wethersfield, CT 06129-0206

Library of Congress Card Catalog Number 94-4493

ISBN 1-880336-04-9

First Edition

Library of Congress Cataloging in Publication Data

Ferguson, Robert
    A guide to rape awareness and prevention / by Robert and Jeanine
    Ferguson - - 1st ed.
        p.   cm.
    ISBN 1-880336-04-9
    1. Rape -- United States -- Prevention. 2. Women -- Crimes
    against -- United States -- Prevention. I. Ferguson, Jeanine II.
    Title III. Title: Rape awareness and prevention.
HV6561.F47   1994
        362.88'3 - - dc20   94-4493

Dedicated to Lavett A. Rayford
with love always.

NOTE TO READERS

The material in this book is intended for educational purposes only. Neither the authors nor the publisher assume any responsibility for the use or misuse of information contained herein. Neither the publisher nor the authors are endorsing any of the referenced resources or products.

Acknowledgments

Together we would like to thank Joan and Art Vance and Mary Lou Siddens for editing our original manuscript and being an encouragement the whole way through. A special thanks to Mrs. Brenda A. Ferguson-Watson for her ongoing support, utmost sincerity, and her leadership and dedication toward making Robert the man he is. We would also like to thank those Rape Awareness and Prevention instructors who have added to the effectiveness of the program: Toni-Jo Menasco, Michael Gibbs, and Roy Simmons. Many thanks to our friend, Beverly Slayton, for photographing the self-defense techniques, and those appearing in them: Toni-Jo Menasco, Cynthia Gregory, Cornelius Jones, John Rodgers, Veronica Ochoa, Oliver and Mericar Ocampo, Michael Gibbs, Roy Simmons, Amanda Naumec, and Shaun Davis. Lastly, our thanks to the many women who have attended the Rape Awareness and Prevention workshops. We have learned much from you.

Contents

Foreword

A great deal has been written about how a woman should respond to a potential rape situation. Much information is available on the causes and history of rape, but there is very little available to aid women in developing more confidence in effectively responding to danger. We hope to fill this void with our book and feel we have made a positive leap in the right direction.

We wrote this book hoping that parents, teachers, and many of those who teach precautionary and preventive workshops for women will use it as a guide to educate others. After conducting countless Rape Awareness and Prevention seminars and self-defense classes for women and following production of the video *"Rape Awareness and Prevention (R.A.P.) for Women,"* we felt it necessary to compile additional information in printed form in order to reach a broader audience.

Most literature on rape prevention stresses too few techniques that can be used when one is threatened with rape. In one instance, there is the man whom the victim knows well but who suddenly becomes sexually overpowering; another may be the surprise attack during the night. Verbal response and assertiveness may not dissuade the attacker, while self-defense may not always be the answer. It is vital to consider each potentially dangerous situation as unique. Your response, drawing on ideas and techniques suggested in this book, may possibly differ in each case.

Use your best judgment. If faced with a situation where your choice would be to give in to an attacker rather than to defend yourself, keep in mind that surrendering is also a practical choice. You did not provoke the crime, you are its victim. No one asks to be raped or deserves to be raped.

We firmly believe that having faith in yourself and learning to size up a situation as or before it happens is one of your most important protective devices. Confidence and education are major factors in crime prevention and awareness. We aim to educate and help you to identify with your confidence level and improve your overall self-assurance and self-esteem. We do believe that men and women together can make a difference with education being the foundation and prevention the goal.

This book is aimed at educating and preparing you to *not* be a victim. It provides you with safety tips, actual experiences, statistics, verbal responses, self-defense tactics, and drills that you can practice and sharpen continuously throughout your lifetime. Keep it in your home and educate your family, friends, and loved ones. Remember to believe in yourself-- confidence plays a big part in preventing rape!

Chapter One
Rape and Its Many Definitions

Rape is defined as the crime of forcing another person to submit to sexual intercourse. Rape can be defined many different ways, but to simplify it, if a person is unwilling and refuses to engage in sexual acts but is forced into doing so, it is undoubtedly considered rape. Most dictionaries define rape using the phrase "forced sexual intercourse", but rape does not always end at sexual intercourse. Some rapists beat their victim, others murder or maim. In fact, forced penetration may be the only foreseeable act performed during the entire assault. Rape is a crime of epidemic proportions, no matter how it is defined.

Today's society does not take the crime of rape seriously enough. Our society has been one that predicts the future based upon current statistics. The statistics that reflect rape and assault are overwhelming. If statistics *are* to indeed predict the future, then we are in serious jeopardy. Our culture sensationalizes sex to such an extent that concern about rape and sexual abuse is greatly overshadowed. With rape occurring more frequently as well as being blatantly overlooked, it has been and continues to be relegated to the "back burner".

It is frequently asked what can be done to prevent this epidemic. The first step is educating ourselves, followed by the education of others.

Initially, we must become familiar with the various definitions, titles, and terms used to describe certain types of rape: *date rape, stranger rape, social rape, and acquaintance rape;* as well as the classifications of rapists to include the *power rapist, sadistic rapist, social rapist, nonsadistic rapist, acquaintance rapist, opportunistic rapist, and anger rapist.* A rapist may be a friend, husband, date, neighbor, employer, etc. Be aware, it can happen to anyone, anyplace, and at anytime. No one is exempt or excluded from rape.

One of the most common forms of rape is known as the *date rape.* Occurring most frequently during or at the conclusion of a date, the *power rapist* expects to have sex as a "thank you gesture" for the privilege of his company.

> *For example:* A man approaches his date for a kiss to close the evening. As she rejects further advances from him, he feels misled, cheated and rejected, so he becomes extremely aggressive. As she continues to resist, he grows more and more violent. He uses all force necessary to subdue his date; pinning her down, striking her, and ultimately raping her.

The power rapist uses his strength to control and force sexual intercourse. He seeks the feeling of being in control, overpowering his victim, and using as much force as necessary to subdue his victim. The more the victim resists, the more the power rapist enjoys what he is doing.

A *stranger rape* is the least common, but the most dangerous. Committed by a *sadistic rapist*, stranger rape is ruthless and unpredictable.

> *For example:* A woman wakes in the middle of the night to find herself being attacked by a man holding a knife to her neck. Brutally beaten, she is traumatized and in shock. She cooperates with his every whim and command. Having no other choice but to obey in a passive and forgiving manner, the woman submits to the rapist in hopes of sparing her life.

In this instance, there is not much one can do to be better prepared to anticipate or avoid an incident such as this. The sadistic rapist enjoys torturing and occasionally murdering his victim, as he derives pleasure from the victim's fear and pain. He is full of hatred, and looks forward to degrading, hurting, and dehumanizing his victim by humiliation and physical brutality. He randomly selects his victims; they may be young, old, ugly, beautiful, fat, or thin-- it doesn't matter. These attacks gain wide media exposure due to the fact that they usually end in grave emotional and physical injury, if not death.

When a teenaged girl is sexually assaulted, it is referred to as *social rape*. The adolescent girl going "steady" with a boy may fall prey to the social rape because she is not yet clear on territorial issues, and is not yet sure who is responsible for any given behavior. As the adolescent woman becomes sexually active, she begins with hand holding, body touching, kissing, fondling, and often oral sex. For a young woman who does not want to have intercourse but has entered into sexual foreplay, she will frequently hear one of the following responses as said by a *social rapist*: "You owe it to me", or "How long do you expect me to wait?" or "You expect me to go this far and stop now?"

Young women often subject themselves to engaging in intercourse when responding to an ultimatum by the boyfriend or by feeling responsible for his sexual state by erroneously thinking, "she owes it to him." In these instances, pressure almost always jeopardizes and destroys young relationships.

The *nonsadistic rapist* has fear that no woman would date or have sexual relations with him, so intercourse is forced. These men usually possess acute feelings of sexual and social inadequacy.

> *For example:* A man who feels he is not physically attractive has been rejected by women many times in the past. Fed up with rejection, the nonsadistic rapist tries to get a woman alone by arranging to have a female co-worker assigned to a project that requires working together after business hours. When he feels the time is right, he makes advances without hesitation and rapes her, hoping she will fall in love with him.

The fantasy of the nonsadistic rapist is that his victim will immediately fall in love with him following intercourse. He fools himself into believing that she bears feelings for him and desires sexual intimacy with him. Moreover, this rapist may have the notion that everything is fine at the conclusion of the assault. He may even ask his victim if she "enjoyed" it.

Acquaintance rape is the most common type of rape. Acquaintance rape, along with date rape, is committed by someone known by the victim. This rapist, referred to as an *acquaintance rapist*, usually admits hearing the woman say "no", but presumes she did not mean it. He feels that if a woman is forced into having sex, she will be grateful later.

For example: A male co-worker gives a woman a ride home. They have dated a few times in the past, so she invites him in for coffee and they sit and talk. Following a couple of kisses, he pushes her back, pinning her on the sofa and raping her, even though she struggles trying to push him off. Fulfilled, he then asks her if she would like to go out again soon.

Many women are raped and never realize it. Bewildered by it all, some women may conclude that "this must be how he makes love," while others blame themselves for having done something to trigger it or feel they were responsible for his behavior.

When opportunity knocks, the *opportunistic rapist* is known to take advantage of any given situation. He is one who does not seek physical conflict, but when he encounters the possibility of self-satisfaction, he seizes the opportunity.

For example: A man breaks into a residence with intentions of stealing valuables. Finding a woman helpless and alone inside, he realizes he can "kill two birds with one stone." Jumping at the opportunity, he rapes her while still taking off with the goods as well.

The opportunistic rapist does not tend to be violent, but if his victim resists, he will use whatever force necessary. He thrives on the suspense, thrill, and excitement of taking chances and experiencing new and risky adventures.

With the many rapists and definitions of rape recognized by our society, the *anger rapist* stands alone. The anger rapist is angry at the world, and enjoys attacking and hurting women in general. In fact, he is as likely to assault men as he is women. Often, he enjoys striking his victim in the head or face while sexually assaulting her. The anger rapist is usually very impulsive and may have a long criminal record.

As stated by an anger rapist: "I continued to commit rapes. Sometimes it was at random. I'd be walking on the street and I would see a woman and say to myself, 'That's the one - she's my next victim'."

In addition to hate or the need for sexual empowerment, the anger rapist may have other motives. As admitted by an anger rapist: "I never gave a damn about anyone's feelings. I didn't have any feelings at all when I was committing crimes, none whatsoever-- except the feeling of danger."

Rape, occurring more frequently than ever, is not *usually* a spontaneous or random attack; most rapes are planned. More than half of all rapes occur either in the victim's or the attacker's home, rather than on the street as commonly believed. Most rapists are known at least casually by the victim. *Anyone* can be a potential rapist. Having lived a childhood of poverty, abuse, or neglect does not cause one to become a rapist. There is no combination of factors that cause a man to rape. The end result is that a man rapes because he chooses to do so.

Character, financial status, appearance, age, or dating habits do not exempt you from rape. No woman wants to live a life filled with paranoia or fear, but she should not consider herself to be excluded from rape either. Be careful in whom you place your trust. Hold complete trust in yourself and your judgment. Take responsibility for your actions so that you are better able to avoid the threat of rape. Understanding rape and recognizing the potential crime ultimately result in better safety. Indeed, the risk factor varies from group to group, but if the statistics state that one of three women is to be raped in her lifetime, do not intuitively categorize yourself as not being *that very one.*

Chapter Two

The Importance of
Self-Confidence and Self-Esteem

Identifying your inner strengths and weaknesses is the beginning in making it possible for you to grow and obtain strong self-esteem and self-confidence (or simply termed "self", for future reference). Strong self adds to your awareness and psychological bearing, and helps you to better deal with the emotional side effects that result from the horrifying experience of being raped. The emotional and mental torment inflicted upon the victim produces an aftermath that seems endless. A woman's dignity is instantly destroyed and she loses faith in society, men in general, and ultimately *herself*.

Take steps now towards bettering and enhancing your self and removing psychological blocks that interfere with self-development. You will become a stronger person who is better able to speak up for herself and her convictions. Strong self-esteem leads to a productive, caring, and happy person; strong self-confidence builds an assured attitude and personality.

The following questions are provided to help you identify with your inner self. Carefully consider each answer. For all questions answered with a "yes", take steps toward enriching your self-development, ultimately reaching the answer "no". Answering "sometimes" or "every once in a while" is considered to be a "yes" answer.

1. Are you unhappy with your figure? _____

According to a 1993 survey taken by the Rape Awareness and Prevention (R.A.P.) Organization, out of 100 women surveyed, 99 answered "yes". Society has set the standards that idealize a beautiful and well-figured woman. As difficult as it may be, every woman should ignore society's demands and ideals and begin to feel comfortable with herself. This creates a strong, self-assured, more "outward self" which is needed in not only confronting a potential rapist, but confronting trying situations, diverse temperaments, and everyday obstacles.

2. Do you answer a question with a question? _____

Answering questions with questions projects a sense of self-doubt and uncertainty. Trust yourself and your convictions, and always make statements with assurance and conviction.

3. Do you feel your lifestyle is unsatisfying? _____

Being happy with yourself and content with your life-style makes for a strong "self". Ask yourself additional questions concerning your relations with family, friends, a boyfriend, or your husband. Be grateful for the things you have and begin taking steps toward building a better tomorrow.

4. Do you have difficulty accepting compliments? _____
Accept compliments with a "thank you". Sincere compliments build on one's self-esteem, assurance, and motivation. Accepting a compliment is not construed as egotistical or vain, but is the acknowledgment and recognition of one's efforts.

5. Do you tell yourself or others you're not good at many things? _____
A woman might say: "I can't do that" or "I wouldn't be good at it, so why should I attempt it when I know I will fail?" You can never fail at something if you never try. Trying is an important step in building confidence and determination. When you attempt something and do not succeed, try again.

6. Do you allow people to interrupt you during a conversation? _____
When being cut short or interrupted during a conversation, do not question yourself or your opinions. As rude as some people may be, let them finish. Many people do not possess the patience of hearing someone out. When the person speaking is finished, follow through with your comment or statement. Believe in yourself and what you represent. Never compromise your self-respect.

7. Do you ever compare yourself to others or to your children? _____
A woman might say: "I wish I had a body like that" or "She's a much better cook than I am" or "I wish I were as intelligent as she." Never compare yourself to others. You can make yourself to be *whatever* and *whomever* you want to be.

Everyday is a new day to improve yourself and eradicate your faults. The day you stop comparing is the day you begin seeing results.

8. Do you gossip or dwell on negative feedback concerning yourself? _____

Negative comments can hurt and damage one's spirit if not challenged. When you are the victim of negative feedback, whether it be from your boss, former boyfriend, a co-worker, etc., be assertive and approach the issue. Getting things out in the open will help settle any differences or misunderstandings.

9. Do you usually need help or assistance in most things you do? _____

When you have many things that need to be accomplished simultaneously, take a step back and accomplish one thing at a time. Having too many things to do at once can cause stress and anxiety. You may begin to lose faith in yourself which may in-turn affect your appearance, attitude, and ultimately, *your health.* Learn to prioritize your duties and manage your time to the best of your advantage. This makes for better judgment and a happier attitude.

10. Do you have poor posture; slouch, or shuffle when you walk or stand still? _____

When demonstrating poor posture and demeanor, you appear to be lacking confidence and possessing poor self. You may feel comfortable, but when viewed by a rapist, you may be seen as his next victim. When your head is held high and you appear poised and assured, you will most likely be someone that a rapist would not want to contend with. Remember, rape is *usually* planned and not spontaneous. A rapist does not want a fight; he selects the weak, vulnerable, and naive.

Answering "yes" to some or all of the above questions does not mean you have failed and lack any promise. Not many women can honestly answer "no" to all of them. A poor self is not developed overnight. It is developed as a result of many errors and shortcomings. Everyone has room for growth. Once you identify with some of your faults, growth will soon follow. On the other hand, you may feel that your self is flawless and not in need of improvement. We have never yet met a person who could not improve qualities about him- or herself.

Many people have a misunderstanding of self and therefore possess a false sense of confidence. Some may feel confident at work, home, and other familiar surroundings. Being in this kind of comfort zone provides a sense of confidence, safety, and security. When taken out of that comfort zone and placed in a situation where there is danger or uncertainty, you must be able to honestly say to yourself "I feel confident and consider myself able to deal with and size up this moment." This type of self is that which will stay with you always, regardless of environment.

Chapter Three
The Effects of the Media

We have all heard the slogan "you are what you eat." In all actuality, you are *and* what you see, hear, and read. The effects of the media are not helping in the fight against rape. They seem to be the fuel that promotes the rampant increase in rape and violence against women.

Movies and television provide a false portrayal of rapists, whether it be their appearance, behavior, approach, or temperament. This causes women to have a false perception about rapists. Thus, women may assume that rape happens in dark alleys with the rapist being perhaps, a large, unkempt man in dirty clothing. Ironically, the majority of rapes occur inside of the home by someone known, at least casually, by the victim.

Advertising

With sexuality being the focus and highlight of most advertisements on television, in magazines, on billboards, etc., the promotion of sexuality will continue to be the forerunner and number-one money-maker for these mediums. When turning on your television, you can expect to view a commercial endorsed with some sort of sexual connotation, whether it be for beer or blue jeans. Women are all too often featured as timid, forgiving, submissive and helpless, the ideal portrayal of someone who is to be victimized. Rarely are women portrayed as confident, angry, assertive, or able to defend themselves. To the contrary, women often successfully *do* defend themselves from rapists and, realistically, are not the victims stereotyped by society and the media.

The lasting effects of the media can instill fear and paranoia in women, and stress their reliance upon men (husband, father, boyfriend, etc.) for protection and security. The degree of bodily harm (aside from the act of rape itself) inflicted upon women and the use of weapons and deadly force is highly overrated. Rarely does the news feature a woman escaping and successfully defending herself from an attacker. In almost every program or news report, the helpless victim is brutalized. With women constantly being featured as victims, many feel they would have an inherent response of being too helpless or incapable of effectively defending themselves in a threatening situation. The media does not build on a woman's self; if anything, it takes away.

Movies and television

Some of the most recognized and admired movies and television shows have promoted rape and other violent acts against women. *Gone with the Wind* is considered to be an all-time American classic and is still viewed by students, critics, and avid moviegoers. In the movie, the character Rhett Butler scoops Scarlett O'Hara up in his arms, carrying her up the majestic staircase to a bedroom; all the while Scarlett screeches, kicks, and claws. She impedes his advances but he ardently continues. In the next scene, Scarlett is shown in bed the next morning, brushing her hair and appearing more elated *at that moment* than throughout the entire movie.

Another negative and widely exposed indignity toward women appeared on the soap opera *General Hospital* which featured the character Luke raping Laura. After being raped, she fell in love and eventually married him. This scene gained high ratings and was promoted greatly by the media and general public. The rape was viewed as a love scene by many and a nightmare by few. The tabloids covered this scene for weeks; giving it praise and the support that did not help in the fight against the reality of real-life rape.

Cartoons aired daily and on Saturday mornings are some of the most violent programming on television. Many action and super hero cartoons teach children early-on that violence, savagery, and hatefulness are part of everyday reality. This volume of crime without consequence or realism instills the belief that violence is just a part of normal living. Movies that would have been rated "X" in the early 1970's are being rated "R" and "NC-17" today. Disturbingly, these movies are in great demand. Practically every video outlet provides video cassettes with outer covers promoting some sort of sexual connotation, whether it be seduction or virtual nudity. The troubling fact is that these videos are some of the most widely rented.

At one time not long ago, a positive, family-oriented motto would have received the highest praise; but not any longer. Now, accounts of someone being murdered, kidnapped, raped, or abused draw the highest ratings, media coverage, and made-for-TV movie offers. Most movies being produced today are likely to contain one or more scenes saturated with sex or violence. It is theorized that rapists and criminals get ideas from these movies. Some individuals cannot separate what is seen on television and what is real. With almost every rape or assault on women being planned, the criminal seemingly becomes "educated" as to how he can effectively accomplish an attack on a woman without being suspected or convicted.

Pornography is a multimillion dollar business and is increasing in sales at a startling rate. Pornography does not cause rape; banning it entirely will not stop rape. Pornography is an insult to both women *and* men. It appears to validate existing attitudes and support the position that women are legitimate targets for sexual abuse and humiliation. Pornography promotes the sexual expression of power and anger which ultimately stimulates an attacker and adds to the many complex dimensions that result in rape. Many rapists accuse pornography of exciting them to rape. Contrary to this belief, a man rapes because he chooses to do so; there *is* no excuse. Pornography is another piece of the puzzle that adds to the distorted picture of how men see women as objects to be victimized.

Popular Music

Today's lyrics are equally as alarming. So alarming, that in some cases, record companies are required by law to attach parental advisory and juvenile warning labels on much of their packaged music. A great deal of current music truly expresses our acquired right to free speech, nonetheless, it also *abuses* this right. Lyrics provide the insight on what women supposedly want, desire, and fantasize about. Degrading women and promoting them as sexual objects is now prevalent. Music videos advertise songs furnished with scantily-clad women acting debasingly, being used, and being taken advantage of by men or the artist(s) themselves. Even though they may take part in these videos for financial gain, they fail to see, or outright ignore, its effect on other women.

Today's songs feature such lyrics as "Do me baby", "I wanna sex you up" and "Let me lick you up and down", whereas until the early 1960's, lyrics of this nature would have been banned by authorities and unheard of. In correlation to the early 1960's and the present, rape has increased dramatically. This has much to do with what was allowed by the media then and what is allowed presently. The degree of profanity and nudity aired publicly has come to the point where it is blatantly offensive and degrading towards women.

Many women are "selling out" for money and glamour by appearing in featured movies and music videos that exploit women in a distasteful manner. For years, women have played the role of "dizzy blonds" or bimbos with nothing between their ears. It should be pointed out that countless women, whether they are blonds, brunettes, or red heads, possess doctorates and hold high corporate and political positions. In spite of their achievements, intelligent, professional women remain stereotyped as "dumb blonds" by the big screen.

Today's society has been molded by the past. In days gone by, rules were followed and laws were upheld. Much of the past is looked at as old-fashioned. Our disturbing present exists because we no longer possess the same honesty, integrity, dignity, and honor as we did in the past. On primitive television, it was distasteful for a woman to appear in much less than a full-length gown, and it was offensive to viewers that such degrading and derogatory material be aired. This great evolution has caused criminal acts toward women to spiral sky-high. Perhaps going back to the past is not such a bad idea. Not that we should give up our independence or rights we have so desperately fought for, but to get back those principles and morals that make for a virtuous and healthy lifestyle.

Chapter Four
Educating Our Youth

If we are to ultimately put a stop to this vicious and demoralizing crime, it is crucial that we first educate ourselves and understand that rape is an abomination only second to homicide. Rape is a malady; a violation of one's body, depriving the victim of both physical and emotional privacy. Yet, not much has been done to educate our youth or society in general of its relentless plundering.

There is confusion as to what constitutes insulting, lewd, and disrespectful attitudes and actions against women. One of the foremost reasons for this is the saturation of today's culture with sexual messages, themes, images, and innuendos. Teenagers view an average of over 1,500 hours of television per year, with much of its substance featuring a variety of sexual connotations and implications. EVERYBODY IS DOING IT. From advertisements and magazines to music and television, teenagers get the impression that sex is more about appearance and attitude than about respect and affection.

To educate the adolescent, you must personally learn how to address the question of sexuality before you can constructively teach your children. When sharing such subject matter as this with your children, speak to them on a one-on-one basis. Help them to understand the emotional qualities that accompany love-making, using everyday terms to identify parts of the anatomy. This will give them a better understanding of what sexual intercourse is, and what it has to do with love between two people. Emphasize what they *should* be doing, not always what they *should not.*

Where have you learned the most about sex? *

13 - 15	AGE	16 - 17
30%	**Parents**	22%
26%	**Friends**	37%
26%	**School**	15%
15%	**Entertainment**	18%

From a telephone poll of 500 American teens taken for TIME/CNN April 13-14 1993 by Yankelovich Partners Inc. Sampling error is ±4.5%. Courtesy of TIME, Inc. Copyright © 1993 Time, Inc. Reprinted by permission.

Rape has been and continues to be severely overlooked; its subject matter avoided and its issue silenced. Rape is not discussed in schools, churches, or at home. It is only discussed briefly after reading about it in the newspaper, watching reports on the news, or perhaps after it happens to someone you know or love. Discussing the subject with both young boys and girls will instill a more respectful attitude toward the opposite sex at an early age.

Rape is on a steady uprise, and until it becomes a significant part of open conversation that parents will touch upon with their children, it will continue to grow worse.

As in some families, sex is considered a taboo that parents feel their children need only know about once they are married. Consequently, teenagers seek advice from their friends, but their friends are just as bewildered. Avoid relying upon books or expecting their knowledge about sex to come from their school, friends, or natural curiosity. Today, sex education classes taught throughout the school system often lack any real discussion of the emotional issues involved, or people's opinions and feelings. Consisting mostly of outdated films and slides with information focused primarily on anatomy, abstinence and birth control, these programs lack essential issues such as date rape, how to refrain from sexual pressure, and the emotional ties and aftereffects when one is coerced into sexual intercourse. Whatever is being taught, responsible sexuality is neither being learned nor practiced.

Many women raped, fondled, or harassed at some point in their lives who informed their mother or someone close to them were told to "Put it all behind you" or "What did you do to trigger it?"

Often the entire objective is overlooked. Now, however, children born into the sexual revolution are beginning to struggle with how to teach their own children about sex. Hypocrisy is a burden that many parents carry. "Do as I say", they instruct their teenagers, "Not as I did".

Of all the mixed messages that teenagers assimilate, the most confusing have to do with gender roles. The stereotypes of male and female behavior have crumbled so quickly over the past generation that parents are at a loss. According to the TIME/

CNN poll, 60% of parents tell their daughters to remain chaste until marriage, but less than half tell their sons the same. Kids reflect this "double standard": more than two-thirds agree that a boy who has sex sees his reputation intensified, while a girl watches hers deteriorate.

Have you ever had sexual intercourse?

	YES
Age 13 - 15	19%
Age 16 - 17	55%

How old were you when you first had sex? *

Under 14	23%
Age 14	24%
Age 15	25%
Age 16	20%
Age 17	6%

How many different partners have you had sex with? *

One	42%
Two to Three	29%
Four	6%
Five or more	15%

* Asked only of those 151 teens who said they had sexual intercourse. Sampling error is ±8%. Courtesy of TIME, Inc. Copyright © 1993 Time, Inc. Reprinted by permission.

Too many of today's youth possess no direction. Their respect is compromised for money, so-called friends, and a good time. Teenaged stripping and the selling of sex at "underground" clubs has become big business in local communities. Denouncing themselves as strippers, these young ladies confess that they do it for the money and that it makes them feel good about themselves. They see it as just having fun and making a little extra money, contending that one day they will look back on it and laugh.

"JUST DO IT." "JUST SAY NO." "JUST WEAR A CONDOM." When it comes to sex, the message to kids today is confusing. School cutbacks and working parents have left teens with a freer and more idle after-school life. Because of this, many kids use this time for socializing more with peers, who may pressure each other into even greater sexual exploration. Because parents are becoming more permissive, their teenagers have excessive freedom.

Indeed, youths *should* be given their independence in order to grow. But as a teenager in today's society, if they do not possess a strong self-image, then they feel they must dress, look, and talk a certain way in order to be accepted, ultimately yielding themselves to peer pressure. Likewise, many parents are in denial about reality and see only the "little boy" or "little girl" in their child and miss the entire issue. "There is no need to inform my 13 year old daughter about rape-- she hasn't started having sex yet," a mother says. This young woman is not going to wake up one morning and magically understand love, sex, or rape. Education *must* start with you, and it must start *now!*

If you are in a position to give advice to someone in their teens or younger, do not hesitate to inform them about sex and crime, and their relation to each other. Share what makes *you* feel threatened. If you find it difficult to explain such a sensitive subject to your child, consult a counselor at a local rape crisis or

*What are the reasons kids you know have sex?**

GIRLS		BOYS
80%	They were curious and wanted to experiment	76%
58%	They wanted to be more popular or impress their friends	58%
63%	They were in love	50%
65%	They were under pressure from those they were dating	35%

Asked only of those 373 teens who know another teen who has had sexual intercourse. Sampling error is ±5%. Courtesy of TIME, Inc. Copyright © 1993 Time, Inc. Reprinted by permission..

family planning center, or notify the Sex Information and Education Council of the United States (SECAS; Publications Catalog; 130 W. 42nd Street; Suite 2500, New York, New York 10036) for assistance or insight on how you can approach it.

Discuss what is real and what is not, what is seen on television and what exists in reality. Even though you may try to screen what your child watches and listens to, he or she sees celebrities and entertainers as sex symbols and role models.

You may take for granted that because your child maintains a high grade point average or has good common sense that he or she instinctively knows what is right and wrong or could handle him- or herself when put in a compromising position. As a parent, do not allow yourself to be overly assuming. Keep in mind what it was like for you as a teenager or youth. Sit down and talk with your child; you may find it one of the most fascinating and refreshing experiences you have ever encountered! It is your responsibility to educate your child and keep him or her forewarned of life's hardships as well as its blessings. Above all, kids need to have their questions addressed. A child who knows about his or her body will most assuredly be better able to deal with the ever-growing pressure to have sex.

By sharing your guidance and awareness with others, you are taking a huge leap toward building a safer and more caring society. Do not keep what you know, learn, and feel to yourself or wait for someone else to do it for you. Educate your family, friends, and anyone else who wishes to listen. Make this world safer for your children. This earth is yours. This life is yours. Ultimately, the choice is yours!

Chapter Five
Automobile, Driving and Travel Safety

Car theft, assault, and car jacking are only a few potential crimes that confront innocent people while on the street each day. These occur more often than you may be aware of or want to believe. When you enter your automobile, do not assume you are immune to danger. Begin treating your safety as a top priority by studying the tips provided. Following these recommendations will enhance your awareness, paving the way toward better safety.

Automobile Safety

1. Always park in well-lit areas and avoid sitting in your automobile for any length of time while in remote areas or in parking lots.

2. Keep your windows slightly ajar or shut and your doors locked; even on hot days and while driving.

3. Always have your key ready and in your hand before walking toward your automobile, and always have your house key in-hand before getting out of your automobile.

4. When walking up to your automobile, look into the back seat before getting in.

5. Have friends escort you to your automobile whenever possible.

6. If approaching your automobile and someone meets you at the door, be careful. Get inside, lock the doors, and drive off.

7. If you see a suspicious person or persons near your automobile from a distance, do not approach it, seek assistance.

8. When getting into your automobile and someone jumps in, immediately try and get out.

9. Do not leave your purse, shopping bags, purchases, or valuables on or underneath a seat. Regardless of whether the doors are locked or unlocked, the majority of criminals are opportunists, and this would only be an invitation.

10. If your automobile breaks down and a stranger approaches, stay inside and lock all of the doors.

11. Never accept a ride from a stranger for _any_ reason. Instead, ask him or her to please call the police for you. In the meantime, raise the hood, flash your emergency lights, and tie a cloth (preferably white) to the antenna or door handle. Invest in a "Send Help" or "Please Call Police" visor for your windshield.

12. When your automobile is being repaired or valet-parked, leave only the ignition key with the service person or attendant. Do not forget to lock your glove compartment.

13. Keep an extra ignition and/or door key and an emergency contact list in your wallet, purse, or somewhere on your person in case you lock yourself out.

Driving Safety

1. Keep a gas can, flashlight, jumper cables, basic tool set, road flares, a map, a good spare tire, and tire-changing accessories handy. A fire extinguisher is also recommended.

2. Learn how to change your tire and ensure that you have a good spare.

3. Keep your automobile in good running order. Routine maintenance and replacement of worn parts in a timely manner will significantly decrease the possibility of breakdowns when you are least prepared.

4. Avoid using self-service gas stations at night.

5. Avoid traveling unfamiliar roads and long distances alone at night.

6. Maintain at least a one-quarter tank of gas at all times.

7. Phone ahead to let people know you are coming, and know where you are headed so that you will not have to stop in an unfamiliar neighborhood to ask directions.

8. Plan to travel with one or more companions, when possible.

9. Never take unfamiliar shortcuts when driving.

10. Do not pick up hitchhikers for *any* reason.

11. If someone is hurt or you witness an accident, stop at the nearest phone to call for help.

12. If followed by a suspicious automobile, take down the license number and drive to the nearest police department, public agency, or well-populated area.

13. If someone tries to force you off the road, do not pull over to avoid damage to your car. Maintain control, continue driving, and get a complete description of the other vehicle.

14. If bumped from behind and you feel at all suspicious, do not get out of your automobile. Motion to the other driver to follow you and go to the nearest well-lit public location where you feel safe, such as a police or fire station, or a hospital.

15. When approaching an intersection, leave enough room between your automobile and the one ahead of you, and remain in gear so you can drive off quickly, if needed.

16. If faced with a potential car jacking, blow your horn loudly and constantly, and move on, if possible. If trapped in traffic, flash lights to get attention.

17. When stopped at a traffic light, use rear view and side mirrors to monitor your surroundings.

18. If confronted with a car jacking, do not argue or struggle with the assailant. If possible, attempt to quickly drive away in the opposite direction and call the police immediately.

19. Keep your driveway lit.

20. Check your surroundings before getting in and out of your automobile.

21. When you drive into your garage using an automatic garage door opener, be aware of someone following you inside.

Travel Safety

1. If commuting to work long distance, drive with a friend or join a carpool.

2. If you travel considerably, invest in a dependable cellular phone or CB radio. Channel Nine is the federal emergency channel and you can use it for help in emergencies. "Monitor 9" is a volunteer program for community services.

3. When traveling, plan your trip carefully. Obtain good directions when traveling to an area that is foreign to you.

4. Consider weather and driving conditions in relation to the type and condition of your automobile.

5. Let someone know where you will be staying, including phone numbers of overnight lodges.

6. Think ahead when traveling and invest in traveler's checks or credit cards.

7. Avoid using teller machines, when possible.

8. When renting a car, ask for one without rental decals so you will not be spotted as a tourist.

9. When traveling in a rental car in an unfamiliar area, ask for directions *before* you leave the rental agency.

10. When checking into a hotel, ask about the security that the establishment has in force.

11. Take advantage of the courtesy most hotels provide by asking to be shown to your room. Ask about exit doors and fire extinguishers, and ask to be moved to another room if you are not completely satisfied with the safety provided.

12. Be aware of adjoining hotel rooms. Ensure the door is locked or request a different room.

13. When someone visits your hotel room, do not open the door. All dialogue should be done through the door.

14. Consider investing in a portable door alarm or door barricade, and always keep your hotel room door locked.

15. If a man approaches you outside of your hotel room, do not go inside your room thinking you will get rid of him. He may follow you or force his way inside. Keep talking and move toward the lobby area where people are gathered.

The tips which you have just covered can better insure your personal safety. As an added note, you may find it beneficial to have in your possession Mace® Defense Spray* or some type of self-protection repellant available to you and within reach. Begin utilizing sure safety on the street, and while driving and traveling.

*Mace® Defense Spray is a registered tradename of Mace Security International, Inc.

Chapter Six
Street, Occupational and Home Safety

In the interest of self-preservation and the healthy continuation of life, it is imperative that you take precautions to insure your own safety. Many persons have an innate trust of others (mind you, this is not a *bad* quality) when approached; of being offered help by a "good samaritan" with your best interest supposedly at heart. In an ideal world, you could accept such offers as benevolent, without the fear of danger. Unfortunately, there is no such thing as an ideal world, and all too often the ploy of "I'm here to help you" is used by would-be rapists who have a perfect crime planned well in advance.

Think of the knowledge you obtain from studying the following safety tips as a life insurance policy; you will never know *if* or *when* you may ever use it. Be it at home, on the street, or at work, the threat of rape is constantly present. Examine each situation and create your own guidelines for intervention if a dangerous situation arises.

Street Safety

1. Avoid walking alone. Simple tasks like emptying the trash or going to the local laundromat are safer when accompanied by a friend.

2. Avoid walking at night. If a situation arises where it is unavoidable, stick to common, well-lit, and populated areas, and always carry a flashlight.

3. Refrain from using automatic teller machines at night and those hidden from public view.

4. Avoid taking short cuts or walking through vacant lots.

5. Walk down the center of the sidewalk. Stay away from doorways, alleys, stairways, and shrubs where an attacker may hide.

6. Try to keep your hands free. Don't overload yourself with bundles of groceries or purchases, and be prepared to drop them quickly, if needed.

7. Avoid carrying oversized purses.

8. Keep your purse or valuables close to your body, and never tie or wind purse straps around your wrist. If grabbed, you could be seriously injured.

9. If your purse is stolen, beware of phone calls telling you where to pick it up. Do not retrieve it yourself, it may be a trap. Let the police handle it.

10. Walk with your keys in-hand. Keys can be used as weapons, and having them out means getting into your automobile or residence more quickly.

11. Do not walk alone when you are emotionally upset, under the influence of drugs or alcohol, depressed, or taking prescription medication, as these may impair your perception and judgement.

12. It is suggested that comfortable shoes be worn in which you can run or take off quickly. You never know when you may need to try and flee a dangerous situation.

13. Walk with confidence and give the impression of control; not of vulnerability.

14. Carrying a self-defense spray is highly advisable, but do not allow yourself to become dependent upon it. (The legal statute for each state differs when regarding self-protection products. Check with your local law enforcement agency for legalities in your state.)

15. If approached by a stranger when in the company of your child, position yourself so that you are between your child and the stranger. Never allow yourself to become preoccupied or distracted by your child; focus all of your attention on the stranger and his every move.

16. Walk facing traffic so that you are aware of cars approaching you.

17. If you believe you are being followed, stay calm and continue walking. Cross the street, change your pace, and seek a safe place. If you can do none of these things, allow your follower to pass you by. If he stops, turn and face him. You stand a better chance in a face-to-face confrontation than with your back turned.

18. If an automobile pulls up beside you heading the same way, reverse your direction. If the automobile stops alongside of you and someone tries to force you inside, scream loudly and draw attention to yourself. Try to run to the nearest place of safety. If you *do* scream, it is often advised that you yell *"FIRE"* or *"NO"* instead of *"HELP"*, since this has been proven to be more effective in arousing public attention.

19. If approached on the street by a suspicious stranger, look for an open or lighted window. Wave or shout as though someone were watching you from inside. Don't be afraid to run up to a house and pound on the door. An attacker does not want to call attention to himself, and the noise may discourage him.

20. If you believe you are being followed, do not return home. This will only give away where you live.

21. Be observant and report descriptions of all suspicious persons or automobiles to your local law enforcement agency.

Occupational Safety

1. Maintain a professional relationship with co-workers, managers, friends, and supervisors.

2. Demand respect when you feel it is being violated. Take a stand, and treat others as you wish to be treated.

3. Refrain from accepting personal gifts from co-workers and supervisors.

4. Keep doors open or slightly ajar when conducting meetings or counseling sessions between male and female co-workers.

5. Always maintain a comfortable distance when working beside male co-workers.

6. Always inform a friend or loved one when you will be working late. Be aware of others in your office who are working late as well.

7. Before using the restroom at work, inform a co-worker of your destination.

8. Use the elevator instead of the stairway and always be aware of your surroundings.

9. Always report suspicious persons or events to security.

10. When traveling with a male co-worker, always clarify that you are interested strictly in business.

Home and Apartment Safety

1. If you have recently moved into a new home or apartment and have lost a key, have the locks changed or re-keyed. The previous tenant may still have a key.

2. Install a strong chain lock to permit only a slight opening of the door.

3. Dead bolt locks which cannot be pried open are highly recommended.

4. Security alarms and timers on indoor and outdoor lighting are suggested.

5. It should not be assumed that a second-story window is safe from burglary and does not need a good lock.

6. Prop a broomstick handle in the track of a sliding glass door to offer increased security.

7. Install a peephole on your front and back doors to permit visual recognition of the person knocking or ringing your doorbell.

8. Keep the exterior of your home well-lit.

9. If you must list your residence in the phone book or on your mailbox, use only your first initials.

10. If you receive obscene phone calls, remain silent-- blow a whistle in the caller's ear or simply hang up.

11. Report any obscene phone calls to the phone company and/or police department.

12. Never hide a key outdoors, especially underneath a doormat.

13. Never leave a key under the doormat, in a flower pot, above the door jam, etc. for anyone; including a friend, neighbor, or maintenance man.

14. Never pin notes on the front door. This is an obvious sign that no one is home.

15. Become familiar with your neighbors and know whom you can trust.

16. Initiate a community neighborhood watch group for mutual benefit and safety.

17. Draw shades and drapes at night. This is especially important for bedroom windows when dressing.

18. When you are planning a trip, remember to stop delivery of your mail and newspaper.

19. If you return home and suspect that someone has broken in, do not enter. It is possible that the burglar may still be inside and you would only be jeopardizing your well-being. If you do surprise a burglar, try to remain calm. Do not get between a burglar and his only escape route. If you scream or move suddenly, you could cause him to hurt you out of fear.

20. If a man is coming into the gate or building behind you, quickly shut and lock the door or gate after you enter. It may be obvious to him that you are shutting him out, but your safety comes *first*.

21. A man with a key in his hand does not necessarily mean that he lives in your complex. Ensure that he opens his front door. This will prove he resides in your complex.

22. Once you open your door, go inside immediately. Avoid leaving it ajar.

23. If your doorbell rings, do not be compelled to answer it, particularly if you are alone. If you do decide to answer, it is suggested you call out, "I'll get the door, Honey" or "I'll get the door, John", as though someone were there with you. Never admit to a stranger that you are home alone.

24. If someone needs to use your phone, dial the number and make the call for them.

25. Be aware of men posing as service personnel attempting to gain entrance to your residence. Any genuine service person should understand and comply with your request for his identification. When unsure, offer to call his office to confirm his visit.

26. If you live in a building that has an elevator, make sure it has not been summoned to the roof or the basement before getting inside.

27. Do not get on an elevator occupied solely by a man. If there are other passengers who get off the elevator and a male stranger remains, get off with the others and wait for another car. If you are alone on the elevator and a strange man (or group of men) gets on, you should immediately get off.

28. When you think you have fully safeguarded your home, go outside and see if there is some way you can break in.

Once you have laid out and created your own guidelines for safety and survival, the next step is to examine each situation as it arises. When in a tight spot or feeling pressured by someone's request, do not feel immediately inclined to answer or help in their dilemma. Follow your intuition. If you carefully consider each situation before making a commitment or even answering someone's request, you stand a much better chance of escaping a potentially dangerous situation.

Chapter Seven

Campus, Public Rest Room, and Public Transportation Safety

Good manners instilled in us as children can often delay our response to a situation in a way that could prevent an attack. It has been proven time and time again that rape is often preceded by a social situation, whether it be at a bar sharing a drink or on a college campus while attending a party. You may become disturbed by a premonition that a certain situation is potentially dangerous, but your social training emerges, telling you you're perhaps overreacting.

Consider every situation as potentially dangerous. Rely and act upon that instinctual feeling of uncertainty. Do not allow your social manners to prevent you from acting in your own best interest or removing yourself from an unwanted situation.

Campus Safety

1. Do not automatically assume you will be safe anywhere within the campus boundaries.

2. Avoid walking to class alone at night.

3. Keep your room or dormitory locked at all times, even if you have dorm security. Register valuable items with campus security.

4. Let a roommate or friend know where you are going and when you intend on returning.

5. It is advised that you not wear headphones when walking or jogging alone.

6. When on a date, never compromise your safety with people whom you do not truly know. Date rape occurs all too frequently.

7. When dating someone for the first time, meet the person at a restaurant, movie theater, or crowded location. Do not make yourself dependent upon your date for transportation. It is all too common for a woman to be driven to a secluded location where she is assaulted.

8. Avoid taking drugs or drinking alcoholic beverages at parties or with a date. This may hinder your ability to make wise decisions.

9. Think twice before letting your date spend a considerable amount of money on you. Many rapists believe that if they spend money on a woman, she owes them sexual favors.

10. Watch for signs of men who tend to become aggressive or will not take "NO" for an answer, even in nonsexual situations.

11. Be candid with your date in regard to sex. It is easier to say "no" at dinner than on your doorstep or in the bedroom.

12. Do not rely strictly upon campus security officers to be there when you need them.

Public Restroom Safety

1. When entering a public restroom, have someone accompany you. Be defensive, aware, and alert at all times.

2. Be careful of setting purses or valuables on the floor when inside of a stall. Items may be quickly snatched from underneath the door or walls.

3. Be especially cautious when using public facilities at:
   ♦ service stations
   ♦ parks, beaches, and recreational facilities
   ♦ fairgrounds and amusement parks
   ♦ concerts
   ♦ shopping centers
   ♦ hospitals
   ♦ airports, bus and train stations

4. If people appear to be congregating in or around the restroom, leave immediately.

Public Transportation Safety

1. If you travel by bus, subway, or any means of public transportation at night, wait in populated, well-lit areas and keep your back to a wall. This will allow you "peripheral vision".

2. Remain alert to any new passengers or unusual behavior.

3. If you find yourself on an empty bus, sit near the driver.

4. When getting off the bus or subway, check to see who gets off with you. If someone suspicious appears to be following you, head quickly for the nearest busy, well-lit building.

5. Do not exit in areas unfamiliar to you.

6. When traveling by train, avoid walking about the cabs at odd hours of the night when few people are around.

7. If occupying an individual compartment, keep your door locked and be suspicious of anyone knocking at your door.

8. During extended layovers in foreign cities, do not feel you must go sightseeing, especially alone. What may be seemingly harmless to you may be the perfect opportunity for a criminal to act.

9. Remain cautious in airports. Watch for someone following you before and after you get off of the plane.

To make effective decisions, develop an awareness of potentially dangerous situations and be cognizant to those factors that may harm or help your decision-making process. Follow your intuition. Understanding yourself, your inner emotions, past experiences, beliefs, opinions, innate intelligence, and social training will increase your ability to make effective and wise decisions.

The past three chapters stressing safety awareness by means of constructive guidelines have been designed in a comprehensive and positive manner. We have attempted to focus on what you *can* do as opposed to governing to you what you *cannot* or *should not* do. It is not our aim to limit your mobility. Simply, use what is effective for you and disregard what is not. The sole intent of this information is to increase your awareness of the problem, which is the first step in preventing its occurrence.

Chapter Eight
Rape Prevention and Split-Second Decisions

How you feel about yourself will directly govern how well you defend yourself in a potentially dangerous predicament. If you are unhappy with yourself or do not trust your own feelings, you will have difficulty defending yourself. If the first thoughts that come to mind when threatened are 'I don't want to make a scene'; 'I don't want to lose my job'; or 'I don't want to hurt his feelings', then you are compromising your safety.

We are all aware of what we do not like about ourselves. To say anything flattering about ourselves is considered by some to be arrogant and vain. Your initial observation and concern in any situation should be of your <u>own</u> benefit and safety. No one has the right to physically or emotionally harass you or infringe upon your space. The prevention of rape is a result of education and the determination to convince yourself that *you are important*. It cannot be stressed enough the significance of caring about yourself and reacting quickly as a direct result.

A Confident Demeanor

Understanding the following personality traits and identifying with your level of self-worth will aid in your detection and prevention of rape:

Body Language. How you carry yourself is a direct indication to a potential rapist of how you feel about yourself and generally how submissive you are. If you have a tendency to walk round-shouldered with your head down generally reflecting poor self-worth, it is the rapist's assumption that you will submit if he threatens you.

Eye Contact. Eye contact is one of the most important elements of an assertive attitude. Regardless of how assertively you speak, avoiding direct eye contact may alert even the most discerning rapist to vulnerability, weakness, and timidity.

Tone of Voice. Verbally responding to an unwanted approach requires a clear, firm voice relaying complete conviction and certainty. Use your face to assist you. Your facial expression alone can reveal your views or disposition when stressing certain points.

Verbal Response. Often an assailant will attempt to engage you in a disarmingly congenial conversation to wear down your apprehension and resistance. Your responses should be direct and up front. Be as brief as possible and give few details. Avoid phrases that require further explanation or invite a conversation.

Dress for Success

The way you dress and carry yourself is crucial when it concerns the prevention of rape. It is an old myth that if a woman carries herself in a provocative manner or wears provocative clothing, she is asking to be raped. When the question *"What is considered to be provocative clothing?"* arises, the answer may differ each time. Despite one's views, what is labeled as provocative varies according to each person's attitude and convictions, whether they are male or female.

No woman asks or deserves to be raped, *at any cost.* Indeed, you can dress conservatively, yet still be attractive. This is not suggesting that you wear only loose-fitting jeans, dresses, or sweaters. It may be that you dress a certain way in order to attract or impress men. This is your choice, and there is *certainly* nothing wrong with it. However, by avoiding revealing attire such as sheer blouses, low-cut tops and short skirts, you avoid drawing attention to your body, which consequently ensures better personal safety for you. It is emphasized that despite how a woman is dressed, men are going to stare, but more so when she is willing to reveal *a little more.* The threat of rape will always be present regardless of how you dress, but present in differing degrees.

Another matter to consider when selecting clothing is mobility if you are attacked. Your possibility of escape increases when you wear clothing that makes it possible to run, maintain balance, kick, and resist freely and practically. Take into consideration your shoes, coat, skirt, jewelry, purse, and long hair where applicable. Ensuring that you possess the mobility to escape, fight back, and react effectively is truly an advantage if ever confronted with rape or assault.

Beware of Acquaintance Rape

There is not much time to think or be creative when handling a confrontation. As seconds go by, you are left with no choice but to react in some way. With the majority of rapes being committed by acquaintances, their inclination to rape and harm is shocking and inconceivable when confronted.

If approached by an acquaintance who displays warmth and trust, most likely your guard will be down, because you may be relaxed and hold mutual feelings of trust. It is very likely that your initial reaction to an aggressive situation of this nature would be passive, retorting with "What are you doing?" or "STOP!". You should treat such an encounter as if being approached by a total stranger. Never question your attacker or the situation. Change your reflex of fear or apprehension into a reflex of action. Possessing this type of preparedness and awareness is your most needed defense, because what you do during your initial encounter with an assailant will ultimately decide the outcome.

Practice through Role Playing

You may ask yourself what you can do to develop the inner strength, confidence, and spirit required for effective verbal responses, self-defense, and fighting tactics that work. The ideal answer is known as *role playing*. The main objective of role playing is to give you an opportunity to *experience* a given or premeditated situation. The more experience you have in exploring the subject matter, the better you will respond to and conquer a situation.

Choose a partner. If you are on your own, act out both parts. Initially, set up scenarios always ending with the question *"What do you do?"*. Act out the situation. We suggest that you try and make it as realistic as possible and that you avoid rehearsing. Think clearly. Do not do anything that would injure yourself or your partner.

You can practice putting yourself in different scenarios everyday, contemplating reasonable and effective responses to handle varying situations. In this manner, if you ever find yourself in a threatening confrontation, you should have the ability to make quick, wise, and accurate decisions to ensure your personal safety. Keep in mind, however, that knowing beforehand how you will react and predicting what your reaction would be in a real-life situation is seemingly impossible.

The following pages illustrate situations that will give you a better understanding of how you can role play and act out different scenarios. It is important that you add your own situations to the ones provided so that you can plan out your responses. Work out a strategy. With this combination of resourceful responses and realizations, you can now make the most out of role playing and physical self-defense techniques.

Scenario One

You have to ride a bus to a predetermined and familiar destination. Once you enter the bus and take your seat, a man gets on and stares at you in a strange and frightening manner. As you approach your destination, you stand and notice the man stands as well. As the bus comes to a stop, what do you do?

You decide to get off the bus, and he decides to get off after you. What do you do?

You decide to stay on the bus and sit down, and he stays on the bus and resumes sitting. What do you do?

You get off the bus and he follows, then you get back on and he follows. This cannot continue. What should you do?

ADVICE: When you reach your destination, be aware of those exiting with you and pay close attention to your surroundings and the possibility of someone following you. When you first exit the bus, stand on the curb near the door and in sight of the driver in case you should need to get back on or need assistance. If you feel uncomfortable or frightened in any way, inform the driver and confront the potential assailant.

Scenario Two

You are on overnight travel with your supervisor. Your job often requires frequent travel and late hours. You have been working for the company for over four years and have traveled both alone and with your supervisor many times.

Your salary is attractive and you realize you could not earn the same salary elsewhere for your experience or level of education. At approximately 11:00 P.M., your supervisor knocks on your hotel room door. He has never done this before. You think it's a little odd, but not to worry, you're still dressed and wide awake. Once you open the door, he says apologetically "I'm sorry. I know it's late, but can we please talk?" What do you do?

Once you let him in, he sits in a chair and loosens his tie. "I may have to let some people go if this deal doesn't go through", he states. "Those who will be laid off first are those with the least seniority. You may fall into that category and I feel terrible - you have been so supportive. You are a very good worker and it bothers me. I'm sorry." He slowly walks to the door to show himself out, but first he approaches you for a hug. What do you do?

As you hug him, he says, "Don't worry, everything will work out." Before you can withdraw from the embrace, he pushes you to the floor, pinning your arms down attempting to remove your clothing. What do you do?

ADVICE: When your supervisor first comes to the door, you should tell him to wait in the lobby and you will join him in a few moments if he wishes to talk. Whether it is day or night, never put yourself in a vulnerable situation where rape could happen, even if it's someone whom you think you can trust. Rape occurs all too often by someone who has your confidence. Never compromise your respect for money, status, or to accommodate someone in need of affection.

Scenario Three

You are home alone and your husband's best friend stops by and wishes to wait for him until he arrives. You have known him for over eight years and have spent much time together. You inform him that you'll be back, you must finish some household chores you were in the middle of. Knowing it will only take a few minutes, you leave him in the living room watching television. Moments later, he comes to ask you if he could welcome himself to a drink. You reply, "Of course, go right ahead."

He then asks you if you could spare a few moments and speak with him. What do you do?

You respond "Sure, what's the problem?" He requests that what he is about to tell you be kept in strict confidence. He shares with you personal matters that concern his wife who happens to be your best friend. Upon discussing a few marriage problems with you, he appears to be discouraged and disheartened. You give him a few words of encouragement and he stands and reaches out for a hug of gratitude. What do you do?

Once you hug him, he then pushes you backwards onto the bed, pinning you down, and attempting to strip you of all your clothing. What do you do?

ADVICE: When he first comes to the bedroom where you are working, return with him to the living room using tact and a firm, direct voice. If he appears to want to stay and talk, walk towards the den or kitchen and finish your chores later. Once you feel threatened or uncomfortable with him being there, follow your intuition and immediately ask him to leave.

Scenario Four

You are in a shopping center parking lot loading your groceries into your automobile. You have your two-year old child with you. While you attempt to seat your child inside, a man approaches you from behind asking for money. What do you do?

Once you turn around, the man insists that you give him some money. You demand that he leave, but he continues to beg. He becomes frustrated and angry. What do you do?

ADVICE: In a situation such as this, you must remain as calm as possible. If you wish, give the vagrant some change and he may leave you alone. If you have a child with you and are approached by a potential assailant, always keep yourself between the assailant and your child. Keep steady eye contact with the attacker. This will allow you to better-handle the situation. Continue moving while talking to the assailant. Put your child inside, lock the door, and position yourself so that the automobile is between you and the assailant. Once you get inside, lock your door and drive away immediately.

Scenario Five

You have a well-figured and mature thirteen-year old daughter. You are happily married to a man whom she knows as her stepfather. Early one morning, your daughter approaches you and informs you that your husband fondled her and forced her into sexual intercourse about three months prior. What do you do?

You refuse to believe her story and insist that she is fabricating the story. Why would she tell you this three months later?

ADVICE: As a parent, be alert to your family's surroundings, your children's activities, and those whom they encounter. Remain open to your children, and communicate with them on a regular basis. Never doubt them as a first response. Show love, concern, and reason, and never take their sincerity for granted. Dealing with rape is extremely painful, and lacking the support of loved ones only adds to their pain.

Chapter Nine
Statistics and Real Life
Experiences

Every woman fears rape, whether it happens in a vacant parking lot, on a blind date, or in a locked room with an acquaintance. But is the fear of victimization rational? To help you answer this question, this chapter contains testimonials and statistics* that shed light on the brutality of rape and your options for survival.

---

* Statistics in this chapter courtesy of the Bureau of Justice Statistics an d the FBI unless otherwise noted. Testimonials are true stories in which names have been changed to protect the identity of the victims and their assailants.

"I considered my boss Roger a friend-- we had been working together for over eight years. Roger had a wife and two beautiful children. Late one night before closing, he called me into his office and closed the door. He started rambling about the past, his personal problems, and how he felt I'd been such a great help to his becoming successful. He walked over to me and pulled me towards him for a hug. The next thing I realized, I was on the floor, pinned down, and my dress was pulled up. I couldn't believe what was happening. It was frightening and shocking. I didn't fight back-- and before I knew it, he stood up and reached his hand out for me."

- Mary, 23 year old Secretary

Facts:*

◆   Over 80% of all rapes are committed by someone known by the victim (boyfriends, husbands, friends, acquaintances, co-workers, and relatives).

◆   One in three women will be the victim of an attempted/completed rape at some point in her life.

◆   The risk of rape is four times higher if a woman is between 16 and 24 years of age.

(* Survey of 200 women by the Rape Awareness and Prevention (R.A.P.) Organization, 1993)

"I am 65 years old and was raped when I was 59. A young man carrying a small package and wearing a brown uniform resembling that of a courier service deliveryman followed me into my apartment building. I told him that I was expecting a package over a week ago and that I had not received it yet. He asked me my name and apartment number and said he'd check the truck once he delivered his package. Approximately ten minutes later he arrived at my door holding a package. I opened the door right away. He pushed me back once I opened the door, knocking me to the floor. Closing the door quickly behind him, he walked briskly through my apartment, checking to see if anyone was home with me. He then got on top of me and questioned me about having any jewelry or money. I told him that I didn't have any, and he pulled me to the bed ripping my clothes off and raping me."

- Betty, 65 year old Retiree

◆ **Age Element:** According to the 1993 R.A.P. survey, 18% of rape victims are over 60 years of age.

"I awoke one night with a man lying on top of me with a knife to my throat. It seemed like a nightmare that I couldn't awake from. I didn't say a word and he didn't move or say anything either. I was terrified and in shock. He began removing my gown and I screamed as loud as I could. He then stuffed a sock in my mouth and I noticed that he was nude from the waist down. He said a few words which I couldn't understand, so I remained still and let him do what he wanted with me. Once he was finished, he grabbed a pillow, placing it over my face, and he fled."

- Terry, 21 year old college student

◆   **Reality:** According to the 1993 R.A.P. survey, only 27% of women whose sexual assault meets the legal definition of rape (differing from state to state) realize they've been raped.

◆   **Where it occurs:** More rapes occur at home, say the Bureau of Justice Statistics, than anywhere else, including on the street, parking lots, or in office buildings.

"I was raped by my fiance' the night before he left for Marine Corps boot camp. Up until this incident, we had never engaged in sex. I was a virgin, and we both agreed that it would remain this way until we were married. We went for a drive out into the country which we'd done many times before. After we were parked for about an hour, he started fondling me. He wasn't the same -- there was something different about him. I told him to quit and he became violent and forced me into the back seat. I continued to tell him to stop and it was as though he didn't hear me. He ripped my under clothes off and raped me. I couldn't believe what had happened - but he acted as though nothing was wrong."

- Brenda, 19 years old

◆ **Who rapes:** While men of all ages and races rape, the largest percentage of offenders are white men in their twenties.

By Race	By Age
White: 59.2%	12 - 20: 21.3%
Black: 26.2%	21 - 29: 40%
Other/unavailable: 14.7%	30 or over: 35.5%
	Age unavailable: 3.3%

Note: Due to rounding off, totals do not always equal 100 percent. Unless otherwise stated, all percentages concerning rape victims include both male and female victims. However, because only two tenths of one percent of rape victims are male, the data should be accurate for women.

"We were living in Indiana at the time. My husband was at work and our two children were in school. My girlfriend's husband had stopped by to say hello. He said he was in the neighborhood and wanted to see if my husband or I were home. We'd known each other for about 14 years, and he and my husband had been friends since high school. I asked him if he would like something to drink, and he said yes. As I was reaching up into the cabinet to get a glass, he grabbed me from behind. I couldn't believe what he was doing. He kept saying 'I know you want me' over and over again. I screamed and kicked him repeatedly, but he was too strong. He slammed me to the floor and raped me. Once he got up, he walked off without saying a word. To this day, I still cannot believe what happened."

- Susan, 43 year old homemaker

◆   **Resisting Rape:** Most women *do* resist with some degree of success.

◆   **Victims of rape or attempted rape who used one or more forms of resistance:** 82.6%

*How they resisted
20.8% physically resisted offender
19.6% screamed or got help*
18.7% appeased offender/persuaded him not to attack
13.0% ran away/hid
12.9% scared off offender
7.9% attacked or threatened offender without weapon*
0.8% attacked offender with weapon
6.2% other

* Some victims may have performed both actions in the category, and therefore may have been counted twice.

◆   **How resistance helped:**

Only 18.9% of women who resisted said that it worsened the situation, while helping it in others. Of those who were helped by resisting:

    39.9% avoided injury or greater injury
    38.3% enabled themselves to escape
    21.7% scared off the offender

"While walking with my boyfriend one evening, three men approached us with a gun. They ordered us both to get into their car. We were horrified. Driving for approximately ten minutes, we stopped in a desolate area and my boyfriend was directed out of the car with a gun to his head. I was raped repeatedly, while my boyfriend was beaten and forced to watch."

- Debbie, 21 years old

"After I was raped, I went to the local Police Station and informed them of my encounter. They told me to sit down and wait. After about 20 minutes, a policeman approached me and told me to follow him. I then had a seat at his desk and he seemed to be more interested in the physical details than my immediate need for someone to care and help me. He asked meaningless questions like, 'How long did it take?', 'In what position did he do it?', 'Did he have a climax?' and 'Were you dressed like that?' After speaking with him, I then had to tell the story to three other police officers before I finally got the needed help I was looking for."

- Sharon, 27 year old librarian

◆ **Percentage of Rapes that Occur:**

At home*: 35%

In commercial building: 7.9%

On the street: 19.9%

In parking lot/garage: 3.4%

At/near friend's home: 10.5%

On public transportation: 1.6%

Near home: 10.3%

In bar/nightclub: 1.5%

Other**: 9.9%

* "At home" includes marital, acquaintance, or stranger rapes occurring in the home and rapes in college dormitories.

** "Other" includes such places as apartment building yards, libraries, churches, playgrounds, hospitals, and parks.

◆ **Percentage of Americans who believe a raped woman is partly to blame if she:**

	MEN	WOMEN
is under influence of alcohol/drugs	39%	42%
says yes to sex, then changes her mind	43%	37%
dresses provocatively	38%	37%
agrees to go to a man's room/home	34%	34%

"My roommate had to go on a business trip over the weekend, so that would leave me alone for two days. In the meantime, my cousin called and informed me he would be in town that same weekend. He was someone I had always admired, so I was eager to spend time with him. Once he arrived, we spent a nice evening together talking about old times, and we retired early.

The next morning at about 9:00 a.m., he appeared in my room with a towel around his waist, wondering where he could find some soap. As I was walking towards my bathroom, he leaped onto my bed removing his towel. I told him to get out of my room and my house. He grabbed me and we wrestled to the floor, but I managed to deter his advances and phone the police. Before the police arrived, he quickly packed up his things and I have not seen him since."

- Dawn, 31 year old dept. store clerk

◆ Why victims report rape - or don't

Why they do:

To prevent further crimes by offender against victim: 32.8%
To punish offender: 20.0%
To prevent crimes by offender against anyone else: 14.6%
To prevent rape-in-progress from being completed: 8.1%
To get help/treatment for injuries: 7.0%
Other* /not available: 17.4%

* (e.g., the victim felt it was her civil duty to report the offensive)

Why they don't:

Private/personal matter: 26.9%
Police ineffective, biased, or annoyed: 21.6%
Fear of reprisal: 7.6%
Incident reported to official other than police: 5.3%
Rape wasn't completed: 2.6%
Victim felt she lacked proof: 2.6%
Other: 33.4%

◆   **Stranger vs. Acquaintance Rape:**

In almost all cases, strangers rape a victim once;
acquaintances often rape the same victim two or more times.

	Female Victims of Stranger Rape	Female Victims of Acquaintance Rape
Number of Rape Incidents		
One	99.2%	55.8%
More than once	0.8%	44.3%
Force Used		
Rapist threatened bodily harm	54.4%	32.8%
Rapist pinned victim down	73.7%	62.0%
Rapist hit, choked or beat victim	43.7%	19.6%
Rapist used weapon	15.8%	3.4%
Victim's Response		
Victim discussed rape with someone	73.2%	54.0%
Victim sought crisis services	24.0%	3.1%
Victim considered suicide	38.5%	26.5%
Victim's Label for Experience		
Rape	55.0%	23.1%
Miscommunication	21.5%	50.9%
Crime, but not rape	15.6%	15.0%
Don't feel victimized	7.9%	11.1%

Source: "Stranger and Acquaintance Rape: Are There Differences in the Victim's Experience?" in Psychology of Women Quarterly, 1988, by Mary P. Koss, University of Arizona; Thomas E. Dinero and Cynthia A. Seibel, Kent State University; and Susan L. Cox, Albany, New York. Reprinted with permission courtesy Glamour. Copyright © 1993 by the Conde Nast Publications Inc.

Chapter Ten
Self-Defense Strategies

Self-defense is defined as the right to protect oneself against violence or threatened violence with whatever force or means reasonably necessary. What some people fail to understand though, is that if the legal limits of protection are exceeded, their *right* can be lost. In other words, you cannot inflict any greater damage than that which you deem *sensible* for your protection. Therefore, if you find yourself in a heated confrontation with a rapist and you manage to kick him in the groin and he falls down, and you then grab a tire iron and smash his head in, you have exceeded your right of utilizing self-defense. Your objective is to escape, not to fight or kill your assailant.

Passive or Aggressive Resistance

When faced with a potentially dangerous confrontation with a rapist, there is no easy way out; however, you do have the choice of reacting passively or aggressively. Using a passive approach is attempting to reason with the assailant, whereas using an aggressive approach is the utilization of physical self-defense measures and the effort to protect yourself from bodily harm. If it is practical to fight back, then you will need to know how to fight effectively. Once this is accomplished, you will be able to better appraise a situation while keeping an avenue of escape in mind. Reacting aggressively is a choice that only you can make. It is recommended that you combine verbal and physical self-defense tactics.

Avoid Hostility

Avoid timid or hostile responses when reacting to a potential attacker's advances. Reacting with a timid response can give the assailant the message that you are uncertain of your feelings and apprehensive of your actions. On the other hand, a hostile response such as "Leave me alone, you stupid bum!" can anger the assailant, escalating the situation in most cases. Responding with antagonistic comments such as this threatens your safety. You are now provoking the assailant, prompting him to hurt you out of spite.

In a rapist's eyes, you are looked at as the victim. By responding hostilely, you are now viewed as the assailant by making him feel as though *he* is the victim. This makes the attacker angry and very defensive. Using assertive verbal response has proved to be an effective deterrent. Be forthright and try holding your ground instead of encouraging a threatening confrontation.

Be Confident in your Choice

Whatever defense mechanism you are able to use, and for whatever reason, it is your choice. Whatever decision you make is the right one for you. Fighting back is a decision that only you can make. No matter what you decide, it is a legitimate choice.

Remaining calm, maintaining distance, becoming confident in yourself and knowing your abilities are all key elements in being able to successfully defend yourself. You may find it difficult to speak up for yourself or you may feel that by standing up for yourself you will anger the assailant and make the situation worse. Your feelings and safety are most important, not his. Don't be hesitant or feel that you are not the aggressive type. Anyone can utilize self-defense and effective verbal response tactics. All you need to do is take the initial step by believing in yourself.

While resisting the physical force of an assailant, do not automatically conclude that you will be able to only "somewhat hurt" your attacker. You must have total and complete faith in yourself in order for your acquired self-defense to work effectively. Your security and safety come first. Another possibility is to pretend or make the assailant think you are weak or that you have been hurt. Make him grow confident when all the while you are waiting for the opportunity to strike and escape. Once given the chance to escape or strike, do so, while always using your best judgement.

Choosing Physical Resistance

Many potential rape situations have been avoided because women reasoned with their attacker and convinced him not to harm them. If you find your verbal skills lacking, you may end up defending yourself physically, using effective strikes and kicks to the rapist's sensitive and vulnerable areas. Always keep in mind that if you *do* decide to fight back, you must attack or counterattack both quickly and with complete conviction. The strikes and kicks must be directed towards areas of the body that result in immediate shock and pain. This way, you can quickly escape and get yourself to safety. Physical force should be used as a last resort, when you feel you must protect your life. Never look for trouble or be quick to use self-defense anytime you get upset.

Taking Action Effectively

When a rapist attacks, he is not expecting a fight, he is expecting you to surrender to him. When you respond with a strike to a vulnerable area, strike him when he is unprepared-- this will take the rapist by surprise, thereby making the strike effective and your being better-able to escape.

To help you remember the seven most vulnerable and accessible areas, keep the acronym "GENTS" in mind: "G" being for groin; "E" for eyes and ears; "N" for nose; "T" for throat; and "S" for shin and knee. If you are grabbed and you repeatedly beat on the assailant's arms and shoulders, it will only aggravate the assailant. A better response would be to drive your palm into

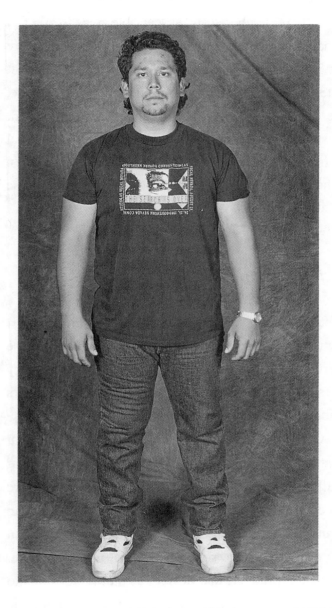

Eyes
Ears
Nose
Throat

Groin

Knees
Shins

The vulnerable areas of the body in which the acronym "GENTS" applies. Please note that vulnerable targets on the body are not limited to only these specified areas.

his nose or strike him abruptly in the throat. Although these targets are not the only vulnerable regions on the body, they are a few of some easily remembered and susceptible areas to aim for.

You may wonder what you would do if your assailant were to weigh over 300 pounds and stand over six feet tall. Actually, it does not matter. Regardless of the man's size or your size or age, attacking the areas mentioned with conviction and force will undoubtedly stun him. You do not have to enroll into a martial arts program in order to exhibit effective self-defense techniques. You possess natural tools of defense and it is your choice to use them if needed.

Self-protection Products

For added protection, you may decide to invest in some sort of self-protection product. Such products include Mace® Defense Spray, PepperGard® Defense Spray, ink spray, a Kubotan® key chain, or a personal alarm. (The legal statute for each state differs when regarding self-protection products such as Mace® Defense Spray, PepperGard® Defense Spray, etc. Check with your local law enforcement agency for legalities in your state.) The list of products available is endless. These protection devices are developed to deter and immobilize an assailant so that you can escape with ample time. It is strongly advised though, that you not allow yourself to become solely dependent upon their use. Consider protection products and devices as *additional* tools to be used as a means of self-protection. Rely on yourself and the natural weapons that you possess.

If you find yourself in a dangerous situation without prior warning, you will most likely be unable to use a self-defense product effectively unless it is already in your hand, especially if it is stored in your purse or out of your immediate reach. Instead of looking in your purse or reaching into your pocket for this device, believe in yourself and use a natural self-defense weapon, be it a knee to the groin, palm strike to the nose, jab to the throat, or kick to the knee.

Be Prepared for Anything

There is no *specific* response for every situation - each confrontation will differ considerably. What should be noted, though, is that many fights and attacks end up on the ground. For this reason, practice ground fighting as well as upright fighting. What works for a small, petite woman will not necessarily work for a larger, taller woman; and vice versa. After you familiarize yourself with this chapter, go back and have a friend put you in a situation in which you can use a *spontaneous response,* a reaction without conscious thought, to your assailant's attack. This is also a good means for practicing your newly acquired abilities.

A single strike or kick may not stop your assailant; you may need to strike repeatedly. With the many different ways to be attacked, no woman knows for sure how or when she may have to defend herself or who she may be up against. Just remember that once attacked, try not to panic. Instead, watch for an opening. If your assailant has a weapon, feign submission and wait for the opportunity to escape by striking one of the vulnerable areas on his body.

Practicing Your Options

Once you begin practicing the techniques provided, research and add new techniques. Practice with friends, relatives, or groups. The more you practice, the more natural it will become for you.

You may practice your natural weapons on your husband or boyfriend and find that the techniques prove to be somewhat ineffective. The reason behind this is that when practicing these tactics with a loved one, you tend to avoid striking or kicking in vulnerable areas with the amount of force necessary to weaken him. It is often best to practice with women versus men. Often, men have an ego that interferes with your being able to effectively benefit in a practice session of self-defense. However, if your partner is humble and sensitive to your needs, he may be a good partner for practicing your self-defense.

Make it part of your strategic plan and arsenal to enable yourself to use effective self-defense both on the ground and on foot. All strikes and actions should be committed and decisive. Remaining calm and focused when confronted with a hostile situation is a developed skill; not an automatic response. If a particular move does not work, try something else. Along with the self-defense techniques provided, remember, while heeding the benefit of their effectiveness, avail yourself of any helpful circumstances over and beyond what is provided.

Chapter Eleven
Defensive Tactics

The self-defense techniques provided are for you to practice, ponder, and utilize if confronted with a physical assault. These techniques are simply *examples,* and it is your responsibility to thoroughly understand their practical application and their legality before utilizing them.

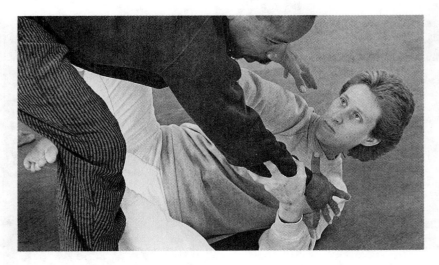

Physically defending yourself requires confidence, technique, commitment, and an inner-strength to succeed and escape. Be a woman in control. Develop the confidence, skill, and attitude needed to successfully defend yourself and escape a physical assault.

Striking: Closed Fist

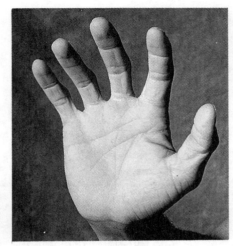

1. To make a fist, begin with your hand open and relaxed . . .

2. curl your fingers inward . . .

3. clench your fingers tightly and cover them with your thumb. If you have long fingernails, loosen your fist slightly.

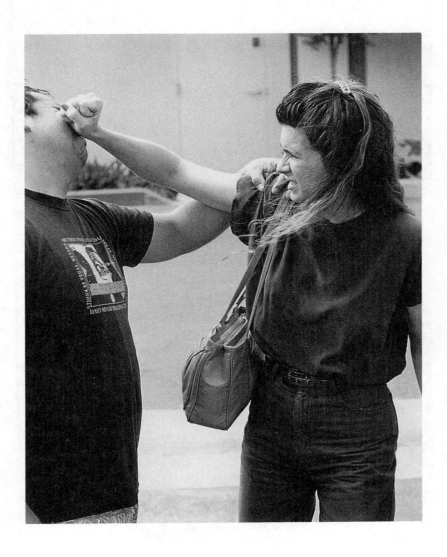

Above is the utilization of a closed fist, striking the assailant across the face. Notice how at the same time, you can knock his hand off of your shoulder while holding onto your automobile for additional support and balance.

Striking: Palm Heel Strike

A flexed wrist or *palm heel strike*, showing the area of the hand to strike with.

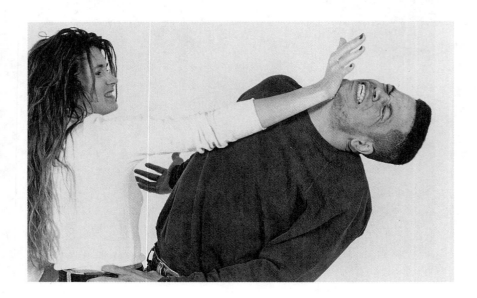

The above technique demonstrates the striking and pushing away of the assailant by driving the heel of the palm into the bottom of his chin. This may cause him temporary unconsciousness if struck with enough force.

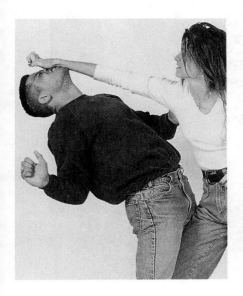

Demonstrated here are ideas for using the palm heel strike. When the groin is struck with a palm strike, you can then grab the testicles and pull, causing excruciating pain to the assailant.

Striking: Kicking

Seeing that the assailant is attempting to get up off of the ground, you may feel it necessary to immobilize him, stopping him from harming you any further. As demonstrated above, strike him with your foot to his groin area.

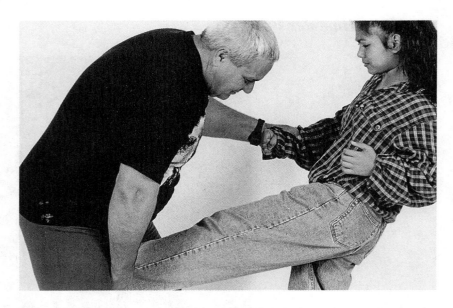

If grabbed by the arm or hand, kick your assailant in the groin area (above) and follow up with a kick to his knee (below). Once the assailant drops his guard and releases his grip, you should immediately flee the area and seek safety.

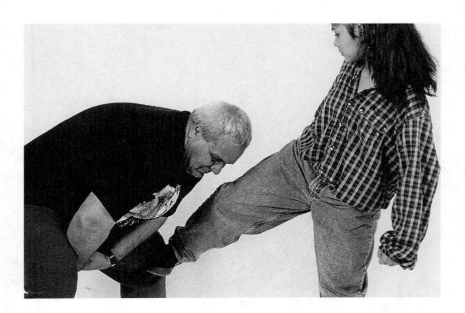

Striking: Hammer Fist

A closed fist or
hammer fist from
side view, pointing
out the striking
surface of the hand.

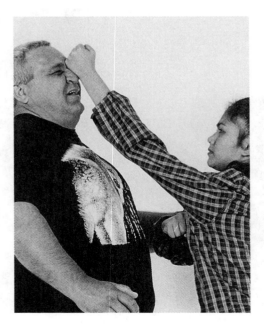

Hammer fist strike
to the nose.

A hammer fist
strike to the groin.

A hammer fist
strike to the jaw,
ear or temple.

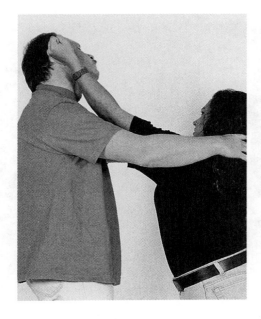

Striking: Heel Strike

The heel can be used to strike the shin . . .   the instep . . .

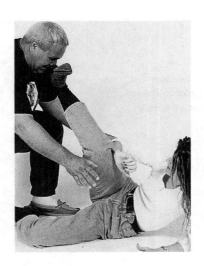

the knee . . .   or the face.

Striking: Wedge Strike

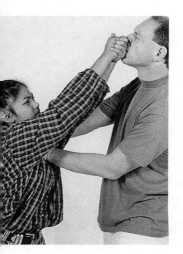
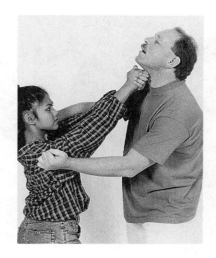

The above techniques are easily applied and very effective. As demonstrated, the wedge maneuver is utilized in a swinging motion against a variety of targets and in many positions.

Striking: Finger Jab

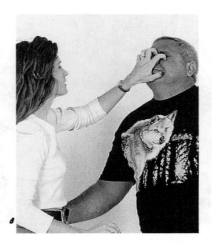

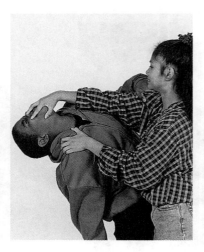

The above techniques demonstrate the use of your fingers to deter an assailant. Note that wherever the nose is manipulated, the head follows . . . a good technique for pushing an assailant away from you.

Striking: Elbow

The above techniques depict innate and effective ways of utilizing the elbow as a natural weapon of defense.

Striking: Knee

This technique demonstrates how your knee can be used to strike your assailant's groin area. Although striking the groin does not always cause *immediate* pain, it usually causes a dull and aching sensation seconds following a strike. You can grab and hold on to your assailant obtaining better balance and stability. Bringing yourself this close to your assailant will make it difficult for your assailant to strike, but will make it easier for <u>you</u> to strike repeatedly.

Striking: Other Options

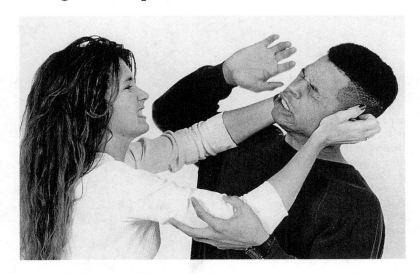

Clapping of an assailant's ears. With enough force applied, this technique will result in the bursting of the eardrums. (Note: This strike should not be practiced on a partner as it can result in serious, permanent damage to the inner ears.)

Biting the earlobe or other soft tissue area of your assailant is also a possibility.

Escaping: Rear Attacks

If grabbed from behind, grab the assailant's arm and either tuck your chin under, or turn your head to the left or right. If your head is neither tucked nor turned, your breathing may be blocked and you may be choked unconscious. Once able to fight back, you can give a heel stomp to your assailant's instep.

If attacked and dragged from behind, hold on to your assailant's arm for balance, and use the heel of your palm to strike his jaw. With enough force, you can easily give your assailant a concussion.

When grabbed from behind, tuck and turn your head, keeping a passageway to breathe. Grab and hang on to the area in which he attempted to strangle you. With this added support and balance, you can use your elbow to thrust backward into his throat (above). In addition, you can use a hammer fist to strike him in his groin area, as illustrated below. You should continue striking him until he releases his grip as a result of your shocking blows to his body.

When an assailant attacks from the front, immediately push forward with your arms in between his, and drive your thumbs into his eyeballs. This will temporarily immobilize your assailant, enabling you to escape or strike another vulnerable area.

Forcing the heel of your palm into your assailant's nose will cause immediate and excruciating pain. Watering of the eyes may result after striking the nose, momentarily blinding him. With one arm free, this is an excellent technique.

If grabbed from the front with both hands free, there are various techniques you can implement. As demonstrated above, use both of your thumbs and push them into your assailant's eyes. This technique will cause immediate pain and obstruction of the assailant's vision. Below, clasp your hands together thrusting them forward, striking your assailant in the throat. This will cause immediate pain and breathing difficulty.

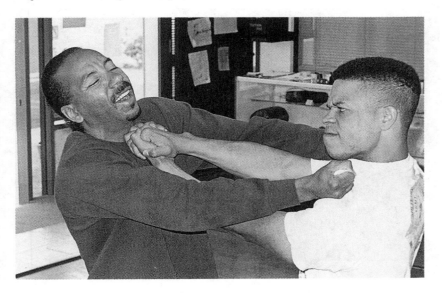

Escaping: Hair Grab

If your hair is grabbed, position your hand between your assailant's hand and your head, as shown above. If he grabs closer to your scalp, place your hand on his hand, but do not attempt to pull his hand off. This will only cause you to pull your own hair.

With your free hand, strike your assailant in the nose with the heel of your palm.

Escaping: Purse Snatching

You can kick your assailant in the knee while using your automobile or other available object for support and balance. An extremely weak joint, the knee takes less than 20 lbs. of pressure to immobilize.

Your purse can also be used as a weapon to fend off an assailant.

Escaping: On the Ground

On the ground, your legs which are your strongest natural weapons, become great tools of defense. Support yourself, preferably turning to your side, kicking out at the assailant's shins and knees.

This technique demonstrates how you can position one of your feet behind the lower part of your assailant's leg, and your other foot on his knee. You can use leverage to injure his knee and knock him off balance.

Escaping: Pinned on the Ground

Ensure your head is raised off of the ground while using your arms and hands to block your assailant's vision and access to you. You can use the heel of your foot to strike his knee, placing your opposite foot behind his leg in order to trip him.

If your assailant breaks through your guard and attempts to climb on top of you, you can prevent further injury to yourself by ensuring your head is off of the ground. Use the heel of your palm to strike his nose or use a wedge strike to his throat to deter him. Place your knee in front of your body, blocking the assailant from advancing any further, and use your other hand to grab him and gain support and stability. This will put you in the position to throw him off to your side using leverage with the aid of your other leg.

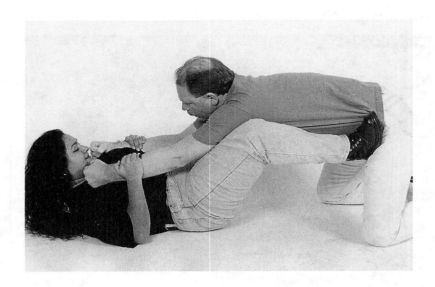

Above illustrates the use of your legs to establish distance by pushing your assailant off and away from you. Once distance is attained, you can kick him in the face and head, as illustrated below.

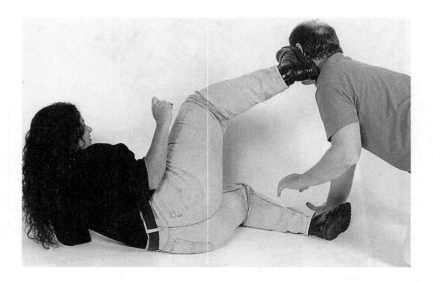

Escaping: Wrist Grab

With both arms being grabbed by your assailant, use your legs by kicking him in the knee. It is recommended that you grab and hold on to your assailant to establish support and balance.

Once the assailant loses his balance, you can strike him in the back, neck head, giving you time to escape.

Escaping: Automobile Safety

If you are near your automobile and an assailant approaches you, try to position yourself between your vehicle and his attack. Strike his nose with the heel of your palm, and rake your fingers downward. You may also want to hit him with the door of your automobile if the opportunity presents itself.

If you are already sitting in your automobile and are approached by a potential assailant, you can use your automobile for support to kick him in the knee enabling you to flee.

If approached by a stranger in an automobile, immediately run in the <u>opposite</u> direction as shown below, to escape a kidnapping attempt.

Self-Protection Products

Self-defense sprays are proven to be very effective. They are great deterrents when properly used, and will immobilize the most aggressive assailant. The only needed elements are distance, commitment, knowledge of the product, and the desire to be safe. They are great tools to carry when walking, jogging, traveling, and so on, but you must not allow yourself to become dependent upon their use. Self-defense and ink sprays, personal alarms, etc., are only *accessories* that add to your personal safety. These self-protection products will not guarantee safety, but will enhance your chances of escaping and immobilizing your assailant.

An assailant is not looking for a fight, nor is he looking to be sprayed with an immobilizing self-defense spray. Ensure you not only carry these products on your person, but in your hand and readily available at all times. You must always be alert and aware of your surroundings and cautious of those whom you are in company with.

If you are walking toward your automobile and notice a stranger approaching you, ensure that your self-defense spray is in your hand and ready for use. Try not to let him get too close to you.

The above photos demonstrate the effective use of self-defense spray. Once the assailant is subdued, immediately leave the area.

Gang Assaults

Gang rape is considered to be one of the most demoralizing and merciless crimes committed. In several isolated incidents, women have even been known to aid in the assault and rape of other women. For instance, a woman may fabricate herself as a decoy in a premeditated assault and will approach another woman in simply needing help or directions. Once she gets her unsuspecting victim alone, she may pull out a gun or lead her to a group of malicious criminals.

If you find yourself in a situation where you are confronted with gang rape, it is vitally important that you remain as calm and rational as possible. Focus your attention and insight on surviving and escaping. If you see an opening, move quickly and be accurate in your actions.

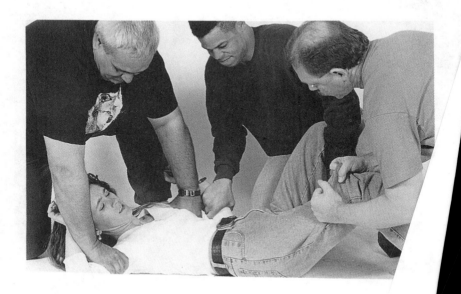

Being pinned down and unable to move or successfully fight back is pr when the odds are two or more against one. Ensure that you not waste panic, or give up while keeping your eyes open for an opportunity to

Youth Assaults

Criminal activity among youths continues to increase and is becoming more common than ever before. Educating our youth should not be just a mere thought or suggestion, but a reality that must be acted upon.

If an adolescent is hostilely approached by a fellow adolescent(s) who intends to cause harm, the goal should be to escape injury. As captured here, this young lady felt her well-being was threatened, and she did what it took to secure her safety and integrity.

Conclusion

We feel that this book has truly filled the void that exists regarding rape prevention and the education of others. It is our hope that you have read, studied, and will utilize this information, not only to educate yourself, but all whom you encounter.

Although we have focused on the *prevention* of rape, knowing what to do when victimized is a key issue that we must all be aware of. If you are raped, do not change clothes, wash, or douche. Seek the comfort of someone whom you can trust. Immediately phone the police or a local rape crisis or victim assistance center to speak with a counselor. A counselor will give you advice and direction on what measures you should take (both legally and medically), and will be a true help in offering immediate and ongoing support.

Do not assume that those you tell will doubt you or feel you asked for it. Likewise, if a friend or loved one should come to you and inform you that they were victimized, support their concerns and needs by helping them confront their distress. Empower her (or him) with comforting thoughts, encouragement, and a strong self-concept.

If there is one statement we must leave with you, it is to live your life as freely, yet *safely*, as possible. The key element in doing this is to *follow your intuition* and to never compromise your self-respect. It is recommended that you base your life upon ethics and a personal investment in educating yourself, your family, and those in need of preventive insight.

Rape is a violent crime being battled by legal statutes, women's organizations, education, awareness, and concerned citizens such as yourself. Men, women, seniors and youths - together we can make a difference. You have already taken the first step. Progress has begun with *you*.

Resources

National Victims Services Organizations:

National Organization of Victim Assistance
1757 Park Road NW
Washington, D.C. 20010
(202) 232-6682

National Victims Center
309 N. 7th St.
Fort Worth, TX 76102
(817) 877-3355

National Educational Organizations:

Rape Awareness and Prevention Organization
P. O. Box 847
Ventura, CA 93002
(805) 986-8425

Sex Information and Education Council of the U.S.
Publications Catalog
130 W. 42nd St., Suite 2500
New York, NY 10036

Index

ABOUT THE AUTHORS

Robert and Jeanine Ferguson are the founders of the Rape Awareness and Prevention Organization, a national organization dedicated to educating women of all ages about rape prevention and self-protection. Since its inception in 1987, RAP has provided workshops for over 15,000 women. Robert, a former marine sergeant and military police officer, has also appeared on numerous radio and television shows, most recently the *Geraldo* Show, as a rape prevention expert. In addition to teaching, lecturing and consulting, Robert and Jeanine are regular contributors to a host of periodicals on the subject of rape prevention.